# Creating a High Performance Team

*Gain the skills of today's successful leaders*

**Rick Conlow**
**Doug Watsabaugh**

*A Crisp Fifty-Minute™ Series Book*

AXZO PRESS

# Creating a High Performance Team

*Gain the skills of today's successful leaders*

**Rick Conlow**
**Doug Watsabaugh**

## CREDITS:

| | |
|---|---|
| President, Axzo Press: | **Jon Winder** |
| Vice President, Product Development: | **Charles G. Blum** |
| Vice President, Operations: | **Josh Pincus** |
| Director, Publishing Systems Development: | **Dan Quackenbush** |
| Copy Editor: | **Catherine M. Albano** |

**Trademarks**

Crisp Fifty-Minute Series is a trademark of Axzo Press.

Some of the product names and company names used in this book have been used for identification purposes only and may be trademarks or registered trademarks of their respective manufacturers and sellers.

**Disclaimer**

We reserve the right to revise this publication and make changes from time to time in its content without notice.

**ISBN 10:** 1-4260-1843-6
**ISBN 13:** 978-1-4260-1843-5

Printed in the United States of America

1 2 3 4 5 08 07 06

# Table of Contents

# About the Authors

## *Doug Watsabaugh*

Doug values being a "regular person," with his feet on the ground and head in the realities of the daily challenges his clients face. It's his heart for and experience in helping clients deal with difficult situations that distinguish him from other sales performance and leadership development consultants.

His knowledge of experiential learning and his skill at designing change processes and learning events have enabled him to measurably improve the lives of thousands of individuals and hundreds of organizations in a wide variety of industries—financial services, manufacturing, medical devices, consumer goods, and technology to name a few.

Before starting his own business, Doug served as the director of operations for a national training institute, as manager of organization development for a major chemical company, and was responsible for worldwide training and organization development for the world's third largest toy company.

He was also a partner in Performance & Human Development LLC, a California company that published high-involvement experiential activities, surveys and instruments, interactive training modules, papers, and multimedia presentations.

Doug has co-authored two books with John E. Jones, Ph.D., and William L. Bearley, Ed. D.: *The New Fieldbook for Trainers* published by HRD Press and Lakewood Publishing, and *The OUS Quality Item Pool*, about organizational survey items that measure Baldrige criteria.

He is a member of the American Society for Training and Development (ASTD), the Minnesota Quality Council, and The National Organization Development Network.

Doug's father taught him the value of hard work, and it paid dividends: He funded his college education by playing guitar and singing with a rock 'n' roll band, experiencing a close call with fame when he played bass in concert with Chuck Berry. Not bad for a guy who admits to being "a bit shy."

While Doug's guitar remains a source of enjoyment, it pales in comparison to his "number one joy and priority"—his family.

## *Rick Conlow*

A quick glance at his professional resume leaves you with the strong impression that effort and optimism are a winning combination. Case in point: With Rick by their side, clients have achieved double- and triple-digit improvement in their sales performance, quality, customer loyalty, and service results over the past 20-plus years and earned more than 30 quality and service awards.

In a day and age where optimism and going the extra mile can sound trite, Rick has made them a differentiator. His clients include organizations that are leaders in their industries, as well as others that are less recognizable. Regardless, their goals are his goals.

Rick's life view and extensive background in sales and leadership—as a general manager, vice president, training director, program director, national sales trainer, and consultant—are the foundation of his coaching, training, and consulting services. Participants in Rick's experiential, "live action" programs walk away with ah-has, inspiration, and skills they can immediately put to use.

These programs include "BEST Selling!", "Moments of Magic!", "Excellence in Management!", "SuperSTAR Service and Selling!", "The Greatest Secrets of all Time!", and "Good Boss/Bad Boss—Which One Are You?"

Rick has also authored *Excellence in Management*, *Excellence in Supervision*, *Returning to Learning*, and *Moments of Magic*.

When he's not engaging an audience or engrossed in a coaching discussion, this proud husband and father is most likely astride a weight bench or motorcycle, taking on the back roads and highways of Minnesota.

## WCW Partners

WCW Partners is a performance improvement company, with more than 20 years of experience helping companies, governmental agencies, and nonprofit organizations worldwide revitalize their results and achieve record-breaking performance.

We are experts in sales performance, organization development, leadership development, marketing and communications—and we don't mind telling you that we're different than most consulting firms you'll find in the marketplace. For one thing, it's our approach—when you hire us, you get us. But just as important, we're people who've had to wrestle with the same issues you have—how to strengthen sales, boost productivity, improve quality, increase employee satisfaction, build a team, or retain and attract new customers. To us, "We develop the capability in you" is more than a catchy phrase. It's our promise.

Our clients include 3M, American Express, American Medical Systems, Amgen Inc., Accenture, AmeriPride Services, Andersen Windows, Avanade, Beltone, Canadian Linen and Uniform Service, Carew International, Case Corporation, Citigroup, Coca-Cola, Costco, Covance, Deknatel, Eaton Corporation, Electrochemicals Inc., Entergy, Esoterix, General Mills, GN Resound, Grant Thornton, Hasbro Inc., Honeywell, Interton, Kenner Products, Marketlink, Kemps-Marigold, Meijer Corporation, National Computer Systems, Parker Brothers, Toro, Productive Workplace Systems, Red Wing Shoes, Rite Aid, Rollerblade, Ryan Companies, Travelers Insurance, Thrivent, Tonka Corporation, and a number of nonprofit and educational institutions.

To learn how you can do amazing things, visit us online at WCWPartners.com or contact Doug or Rick toll free at 1-888-313-0514.

# Preface

Dramatic change is buffeting our organizations in ways that we have never experienced in our history. And, our organizations are increasingly complex systems strung far and wide, both geographically, and across businesses. Old style "command and control" mechanisms are becoming increasingly irrelevant and ineffective, and the need for close communication and collaboration is challenging our leaders more than ever before.

This book is designed to provide a step-by-step guide and inside look at the specific tasks that need to be orchestrated in order to lead teams in today's organization. The information you'll find here draws from more than 50 years of research and knowledge and ties it together in a short, to-the-point set of strategies, action steps, and tools to help you as a leader assess the status of your needs and quickly begin to take the leadership actions needed to start or revitalize a team. This book is a labor of love and addresses some of the reasons why we got into the business of helping businesses and leaders grow many years ago.

We want to give a special thank you to Meg Leach, our colleague and friend. Meg's team knowledge and skill are reflected throughout this book.

Sincerely,

Doug and Rick

## Learning Objectives

Complete this book, and you'll know how to:

1) Diagnose the stage of your team's development and use that information to guide your leadership strategy to bring the team to higher performance.

2) Continuously improve your leadership skills, select the right team members for the task, establish the team's purpose, and ensure fit with the organization's needs.

3) Lead your team through the stages of development to realize the successful performance required by the organization.

4) Lead a "problem team" or "broken team" to effective performance.

5) Revitalize a "tired team" and create a "virtual team."

## Workplace and Management Competencies mapping

For over 30 years, business and industry has utilized competency models to select employees. The trend to use competency-based approaches in education and training, assessment, and development of workers has experienced a more recent emergence within the Employment and Training Administration (ETA), a division of the United States Department of Labor.

The ETA's General Competency Model Framework spans a wide array of competencies from the more basic competencies, such as reading and writing, to more advanced occupation-specific competencies. The Crisp Series finds its home in what the ETA refers to as the Workplace Competencies and the Management Competencies.

*Creating a High Performance Team* covers information vital to mastering the following competencies:

### Workplace Competencies:

▶ Teamwork

### Management Competencies:

▶ Supporting Others

▶ Motivating & Inspiring

▶ Clarifying Roles & Objectives

▶ Managing Conflict & Team Building

For a comprehensive mapping of Crisp Series titles to the Workplace and Management competencies, visit www.CrispSeries.com.

# About the Crisp 50-Minute Series

The Crisp 50-Minute Series was designed to cover critical business and professional development topics in the shortest possible time. Our easy-to-read, easy-to-understand format can be used for self-study or for classroom training. With a wealth of hands-on exercises, the 50-Minute books keep you engaged and help you retain critical skills.

## *What You Need to Know*

We designed the Crisp 50-Minute Series to be as self-explanatory as possible. But there are a few things you should know before you begin the book.

### Exercises

Exercises look like this:

### EXERCISE TITLE

Questions and other information would be here.

Keep a pencil handy. Any time you see an exercise, you should try to complete it. If the exercise has specific answers, an answer key will be provided in the appendix. (Some exercises ask you to think about your own opinions or situation; these types of exercises will not have answer keys.)

### Forms

A heading like this means that the rest of the page is a form:

## FORMHEAD

Forms are meant to be reusable. You might want to make a photocopy of a form before you fill it out, so that you can use it again later.

# A Note to Instructors

We've tried to make the Crisp 50-Minute Series books as useful as possible as classroom training manuals. Here are some of the features we provide for instructors:

- ▶ PowerPoint presentations
- ▶ Answer keys
- ▶ Assessments
- ▶ Customization

## PowerPoint Presentations

You can download a PowerPoint presentation for this book from our Web site at www.CrispSeries.com.

## Answer keys

If an exercise has specific answers, an answer key will be provided in the appendix. (Some exercises ask you to think about your own opinions or situation; these types of exercises will not have answer keys.)

## Assessments

For each 50-Minute Series book, we have developed a 35- to 50-item assessment. The assessment for this book is available at www.CrispSeries.com. *Assessments should not be used in any employee-selection process.*

## Customization

Crisp books can be quickly and easily customized to meet your needs—from adding your logo to developing proprietary content. Crisp books are available in print and electronic form. For more information on customization, see www.CrispSeries.com.

# The Task of

# Building a Team

“
*No one can whistle a symphony. It takes an orchestra to play it…”*

–H. E. Luccock

## *In this part:*

▶ The value of teams

▶ The difference between groups and teams

▶ The stages of team development; some pitfalls when they don't develop constructively

▶ Working with teams in a variety of real-world situations—new teams, problem teams, teams that are tired or virtual

▶ The language of teams

# The Value of Teams

In Antarctica the sun sets at the start of winter, and temperatures can dip below –100°. No planes can land at the Amundsen-Scott South Pole Station; it is cut off from the rest of the world. Its crew members must depend on each other until the sun rises six months later.

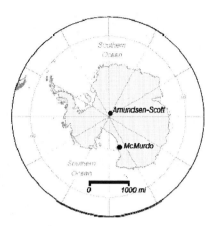

Dr. Jerri Nielsen Fitzgerald was the only doctor at the station in the winter of 1999. During a routine self-exam she discovered what she thought might be cancer but she needed a biopsy to be certain.

The National Science Foundation arranged for a U.S. Air Force plane launched from New Zealand to overfly the pole. As the plane neared, members of the station crew went out on the ice and lit fires in barrels to mark a drop zone. Six parachutes drifted out of the darkness, bringing bundles of supplies and medication.

With the help of stateside doctors consulting via satellite link, Dr. Nielsen trained a team to help her perform the biopsy and the cancer treatments that followed, such as staining slides, using an electronic microscope, and administering IV chemotherapy. The members of the team had no prior medical experience—they included a welder, a maintenance worker, and a computer technician, among others.

The treatments helped, but what she really needed was a hospital. So several weeks before the official safe-flying date, when temperatures bobbed up to a balmy –60°, the New York Air National Guard refueled at McMurdo Station on the coast, and landed a specially equipped plane at the pole. Twenty-two minutes later, the doctor and another injured team member were en route to a U.S. hospital.

How many teams played a role in this story? They include the NSF, the U.S. Air Force, the N.Z. Air Force, the crew that went out on the ice, the doctors back home, the "medics" at the station, the crew at McMurdo, and the New York ANG. No doubt there are many more teams behind the scenes who also contributed.

Most of us will never have to rely on such extraordinary life-saving teams. In fact, if you've ever been a part of a team, there were probably days when you wondered, "Why bother? I could do this faster myself."

Maybe for that project, on that day, it was true. But in most cases, working with a team produces a better, more complete, more effective result. Teams offer a richness that one person can't give to even a small project.

## *Resistance to Teams*

There is often a resistance to teams in corporate America. Resistance is usually stated as a bias toward Individualism. We like the idea of being The Best and The Brightest. If there's a whole group, how will everyone know who's on top?

There's also resistance because teams take time. It's faster to make decisions alone. Teams are slow. Everyone wants to talk and share their knowledge, expertise, and opinion. Organizations don't reward team achievement in the same way they reward individuals with accolades, raises, and promotions. So why encourage teams?

A well-chosen team offers more expertise and knowledge than even a very smart individual can. Teams give perspective from different levels and disciplines of the organization. There is a richness of ideas and thinking styles. All of this does take more time. But the product of a good team far surpasses the contribution of a person working alone. Teams also change the dynamics of the whole organization through the collaborations that develop and the quality of projects delivered.

> *Never doubt that a small group of thoughtful, committed people can change the world. Indeed, it is the only thing that ever has."*
>
> **–Margaret Mead**

"Jack, I must have you on my team."

# The Definition of Team

A group is not a team.

When we use the word *team* we are not talking about a collection of people who work in the same office or even people with the same titles who report to the same boss. A team implies people coming together for a common purpose. They may be from different departments, with different titles, different educational backgrounds, disciplines, and expertise, but they come together to accomplish a specific goal. They are focused on a common outcome, committed to finding the best solution, and committed to each other.

## Team

*A small number of people with complementary skills, committed to a common purpose, set of performance goals, and approach for which they hold themselves mutually accountable.*

*Jon R. Katzenbach and Douglas Smith,*
*Harvard Business Review,*
*March–April 1993*

## BEST TEAM EXPERIENCE

1. What was the best team with which you ever worked?

   _____

2. Who was on the team?

   _____

3. What was the reason for the team?

   _____

4. What made it work so well?

   _____

   _____

5. Why is it so memorable?

   _____

   _____

6. What was the mix of people?

   _____

   _____

7. What was the energy level?

   _____

   _____

8. What was the outcome?

   _____

   _____

9. What did you learn about working in teams from this experience?

   _____

   _____

   _____

# Stages of Team Development

In 1965, Dr. Bruce Tuckman created a model to describe group development.[1] Many have "renamed" the stages of development over the years, but essentially the same descriptions of the challenges and the necessary tasks carry through today. We have chosen to work within the original descriptions for the sake of consistency. The stages are:

**F**orming

**S**torming

**N**orming

**P**erforming

**A**djourning

## *Forming*

The startup stage is called Forming. Group members get acquainted, begin to build trust, and check out the leader's ability to manage the group. There is mix of excitement, optimism, and fear as the group begins to create a plan for achieving the potential of the group.

### Tasks for This Stage

▶ Get acquainted and build relationships.

▶ Agree on a common purpose that describes what they will do.

▶ Agree on how they will do that work.

▶ Establish goals, roles, and procedures.

---

[1] Tuckman, B.W., & Jensen, M.A. (1977). Stages of small-group development revisited. *Group & Organizational Management, 2*:419–427.

## Storming

The Storming stage can produce three very different groups:

▶ **Passive-Aggressive Group** – These are the unhappy, seething, uncooperative, no-progress groups. Group members are often individuals moving alone toward unclear goals. They choose not to share information and then complain about how unproductive the group is.

▶ **Aggressive Group** – There is also the group that loudly protests. They let everyone know how unhappy they are but they refuse to participate in the activities of the group. It is a conflicting group of stars, each of whom works without regard for the good of the group.

What these two types have in common is conflict: sometimes loud and vicious, sometimes quiet and indirect. In both cases they are showing their unhappiness with the group. As the leader of such a group, it is your job to redirect its energy.

▶ **Assertive Group** – An insightful leader takes all the diversity of thought, experience, and style in an assertive group and channels that energy toward finding wildly creative solutions. There will be conflicts; however, such conflicts will be seen as catalysts for change.

### Tasks for This Stage

▶ Work out ways of dealing with conflict and differences of opinion.

▶ Use conflicts and differences in styles, expertise, and knowledge to create the best outcomes.

▶ Establish how "we" will work through our differences, and who will be influential in the team.

## Norming

Norming is the somewhat peaceful stage that follows the Storm. It is a time when the culture (how we do things around here) is clearly defined—rules, roles, and relationships—and the leader works to provide the productive environment the team needs. The Norming stage happens when a small group of people "have a variety of skills and are committed to a common purpose, set of performance goals and approach for which they hold themselves mutually accountable come together."

### Tasks for This Stage

▶ Push ourselves to higher performance.

▶ Enjoy the new-found peace and productivity, but we don't get complacent.

# Performing

In the Performing stage, the focus is on achieving goals through collaboration. There is an urgency to get to the finish line and a sense of relief when it is reached.

### Tasks for This Stage

▶ Produce outcomes are consistent with the team's purpose.

▶ Keep up the energy level.

# Adjourning

Adjourning wasn't one of Dr. Tuckman's original stages. It was added later because the acknowledgment and celebration of the completion of a special task is also important. For intact teams, it is very likely that they will repeat this cycle (Forming, Storming, Norming, Performing, Adjourning) many times over the course of their time together. So, having a celebration and reviewing "how we're doing" is essential for ongoing team building.

For single-project teams, Adjourning allows a sense of pride and accomplishment. But it also brings to a close the project camaraderie. That makes the marking of Adjournment important for this team and for others in the organization. It sends the message that the organization values teamwork.

### Tasks for This Stage

▶ Celebrating

▶ Cataloging the ingredients for success for use the next time

▶ Saying good-bye to the project and/or the team

## *Repeating the Cycle*

For permanent teams, these stages may repeat themselves several times. Corporate downsizing may change some teams that were performing at their peak. Teams might be so reduced in size that they needed to be "Re-formed." They will have to Storm again, find new Norms, and Perform up to expectations of the original team charter or purpose. Understanding the tasks in each stage can help leaders speed up this process and return to the Performing stage much more quickly.

> *When a team outgrows individual performance and learns team confidence, excellence becomes a reality."*
>
> **–Joe Paterno**

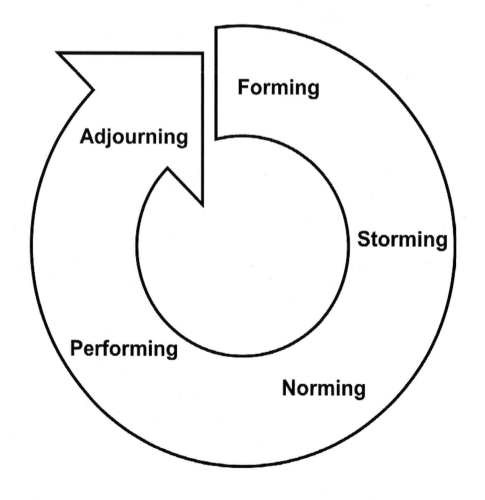

# Types of Teams

Sometimes the task of building a team really means taking a tired, dormant, unfocused group of people and pushing, begging, and exhorting them to produce something beyond themselves. Or you may be asked to gather a group of people from very different disciplines and appeal to their sense of organizational commitment to perform together. If you are very lucky in your career, you will have at least one chance to create a new team and lead it to a compelling goal. In each case you will need to understand the types of teams you are working with and how to move them effortlessly through their stages of development.

In this section, we'll look at four types of teams:

▶ New teams

▶ Problem teams

▶ Tired teams

▶ Virtual teams

 *None of us, including me, ever do great things. But we can all do small things, with great love, and together we can do something wonderful."*

**−Mother Teresa**

## New Teams

> ### CASE STUDY: Creating a New Team
>
> "The caller identified himself as Mr. Andy Zaleta of Korn-Ferry, the largest executive headhunting firm in the world. He asked if I'd be interested in establishing and directing an international design facility for one of the world's largest non-American auto manufacturers. Along with continuing to be an active designer, I would help locate the site—for the potentially ideal creative environment—(anywhere in America I felt appropriate), find and work with an architect, hire a select staff, and create a unique organization and methodology for designing real cars for the real world."
>
> –*Creative Priority* by Jerry Hirschberg, Founder and President,
> Nissan Design International

That's team creation at its finest and most exciting! All Jerry Hirschberg had to do was say, "Yes," and then choose a location anywhere in America, build a state-of-the-art research facility, and staff it with the very best people he could find—to build cars Americans would buy. The purpose was very clear. Hirschberg's next task was to find the people.

Very few of us will ever have an opportunity like the one Jerry Hirschberg was offered. At the time he was the Chief Designer at Buick. When he got this call he thought it was such an outrageous idea that he hung up on the caller, thinking someone was playing a joke on him. He discovered that it was a real offer, and one he couldn't turn down. Eventually, he also used this fertile environment for designing children's furniture, high-end boats, and computers. And he learned about creating environments for optimism, originality, teamwork, and output.

### Challenges of the New Team

- ▶ Create a clear purpose.
- ▶ Choose the right team mix.
- ▶ Build team spirit.
- ▶ Know where to begin.
- ▶ Find support within the organization.

# *Problem Teams*

> ### ▓▓▓▓ CASE STUDY: Fixing a Problem Team ▓▓▓▓
>
> Andrea was very excited about managing the sales team. She'd met all of the team members, but needed a bit more insight into the group. Her boss told her, "They're a very independent, driven, competitive crowd. They were not a problem in the past but there has been more dissension lately and that seems to be affecting sales." He'd been getting calls about sales execs encroaching on others' territories and saying unflattering things about team members to customers. Customers complained of incompetence and poor deliveries.
>
> The strained situation was made worse by new directives to meet difficult goals. Three people left the company and the sales people who remained weren't meeting sales quotas. The boss needed Andrea to come up with some creative ideas for getting the product out there. And, if she could also help them to be nicer to each other—that'd be good too. He wished her luck.

## Challenges of Repairing a Troubled Team

▶ Find a common purpose.

▶ Create team spirit and commitment to work together.

▶ Ensure personal responsibility.

## *Tired Teams*

---

### CASE STUDY: Revitalizing a Tired Team

The 12 physicians who made up the West Wind Medical Clinic were very successful. They were a friendly group who socialized with all the staff and family members. They hosted a yearly benefit for children's sports and were considered members in good standing in the community. The physicians met monthly to review finances and staffing and they referred to each other on a regular basis. Except for adding a few specialty practices and additional administrative staff, they had not changed significantly since they opened the practice 12 years before.

Now, however, there was a rumor that the local medical school was considering opening a new clinic four blocks away. Those physicians would have many more resources available to them and could draw patients away.

As soon as the rumor hit the clinic, people were knocking on Dr. West's door with their concerns and asking what he was planning to do about this threat of competition. While he was one of the 2 physicians who started the clinic, he didn't really see himself as a CEO. His role was more that of a lead doctor. He was comfortable reviewing charts for other physicians, giving advice about patients, and fairly comfortable working with the clinic's accountants on a quarterly basis. But he didn't have answers for this problem and he didn't think the other physicians did either. They hadn't really ever had to think about the future of the clinic. It just seemed to run itself. Now there was concern.

---

### Challenges of Revitalizing

▶ Find a new strategic purpose.

▶ Find new leadership.

▶ Create team spirit and commitment to work together.

▶ Encourage personal responsibility.

# *Virtual Teams*

---

## CASE STUDY: Establishing a Virtual Team

Two of the team members were in Japan, three were in California, two more in Colorado, and their leader was located in Kansas. Communicating as a group could be difficult. They were in different time zones, one spoke very little English, and one was working part-time from her home while she cared for a new baby.

Businesses are now global. We sell to and buy from countries we hadn't heard of even five years ago. But with high travel costs, fewer employees, and people who work part-time, we need to find ways keep people at their desks *and* connected to the world.

---

## Challenges

▶ Learn to work together and be productive without direct personal contact.

▶ Discover a new way of being a team.

▶ Learn new technology.

▶ Understand differences in culture and global issues (time zones, holidays, travel, and so on).

▶ Maintain personal connections.

# The Language of Teams

One of the challenges that all these teams have in common is language. Each organization has its own definitions of mission, vision, and goals. For clarification, we offer this vocabulary list for you:

▶ Values

▶ Purpose

▶ Vision

▶ Strategies

▶ Goals

▶ Tactics

## Values

Values are the words and statements that guide the behaviors of groups and organizations. Here are some examples:

▶ Achievement

▶ Integrity

▶ Belonging

▶ Courage

▶ Learning

## Purpose

The reason the group exists; its reason for being. The Purpose statement is very clear, very short, very directive. Here are some examples:

▶ Provide the organization with accurate accounting of their finances.

▶ Manage our assets.

▶ Deliver support to the finance department.

The purpose statement should be apparent to everyone and everyone's job should be supportive of the purpose statement. There is an exercise in the part entitled "The Leader of Teams" that will help you clarify the purpose for your team.

## Vision

This is the group's image of their best possible future. The vision is the exciting-but-realistic dream of what the team can do with its purpose. Here are some examples:

- ▶ This team will find a workable application of solar energy…
- ▶ We will create a world class toy factory in…

The vision statement should energize everyone on the team and help them keep a focus on the future. There is an exercise in the part entitled "Revitalizing the Inactive Team and Creating the Virtual Team" to help you create a vision for your team.

## Strategies

These are the major categories of work that will need to be done to achieve the vision. Strategy suggests a "stream of actions" that will take you in a particular direction and allow you to fulfill your vision. There are many different ways to go, so your strategy needs to be considered in terms of efficiencies, competitive pressures, use of talents, and positioning, as well as other possible considerations.

## Goals

These are the measures or statements of intent that give the team the direction and scope in their planning process.

Because vision statements need to be specific, you will probably have only 4–5 goals. If you have more than that your vision may be too broad.

## Tactics

These spell out the work of the strategies and describe the actions to be taken, the resource needs, accountabilities, and timeframes.

Tactics help each person on the team to understand exactly what they need to do, in what amount of time, and what help they can get.

# Part Summary

You may have the great good fortune to create a new team. You'll get to choose all the members of your team, lead them smoothly and quickly through each stage of team development, achieve the goals, and then adjourn joyfully. Unfortunately, you may be asked to fix a problem team that has formed but is stuck in the Storming stage with conflicts and lack of enthusiasm. There will probably be an opportunity in your career to revitalize a tired team that has gotten to the Norming stage and can't get past that to the Performing stage to deliver the vision they promised. In this high tech world you may also be asked to start up a Virtual team and lead them through all the stages without ever seeing them in person. If you have been a leader of a team that has been together for a long time, you may be aware that you have gone through each of the stages several times as new team members and projects come along. Each of these teams has the potential of bringing great value to the organization. The following discussion reviews the ways the different types of teams move through each of the stages of development and how you, as their leader, can help them to do that to create the best possible outcomes.

# The Leader of

# Teams

> **Coming together is a beginning, staying together is progress, and working together is success.**
>
> **–Henry Ford**

## *In this part:*

▶ The qualities you will need to effectively lead a team

▶ The importance of identifying a team's purpose, and how to go about it

▶ How to choose the best team for your purpose

# So, You're Going to Lead a Team

---

**CASE STUDY: The New Leader**

Paul was hired by the organization that was first on his list after college. After a little time spent in a small cube they promoted him, moved him to an extra large cube, and gave him an assistant and a direct report. Paul did so well on a couple of projects they offered him a "real" office and promotion and *a team*! He was thrilled. How hard could it be to put together a team and produce a product in six months?

---

That may not be your story but the question still remains: Do you have what it takes to lead at team? Do you have the skills to start from nothing and build a productive, collaborative team? Are you up for the challenge of repairing a damaged or weary team? Being asked to lead a team is a big career step. For some it means going from peer or co-worker to becoming the boss of those co-workers. It means you've been singled out as someone who has credibility and leadership skills. In the next few parts of this book you'll have an opportunity to assess your team leader skills, to learn about the value of teams, to discover how to lead new teams, old, tired teams, virtual teams, and even the problem teams across all stages of their development.

Historically, bosses got groups to work together by ultimatum. "We need this—make it happen." Or worse, the boss just gave the directive and employees did her bidding. Because we now understand the wealth of experience and knowledge a team can bring to a project or issue; we use the team approach to resolve even the most difficult organizational issues. The team approach requires a leader who understands the value of having different voices come together to achieve a clear goal. An effective team leader is an expert in encouraging participation and spirited debate to get the best possible solution. A successful team leader isn't concerned about position as much as he or she is concerned about making use of all talents to ensure the best outcome for the organization.

# BEST TEAM LEADER

Respond to the questions below, and use them to help you "unpack" the elements of effective team leadership that are meaningful to you.

1. Who is the best leader you ever had?

   _____

2. What was it about this person (characteristics or qualities) that made you want to be part of whatever team they were leading?

   _____

   _____

   _____

   _____

3. What did this person do that made the team so successful and satisfying for you?

   _____

   _____

   _____

   _____

4. What conclusions can you draw from your experience with this leader that can guide your own effectiveness as you move into team leadership?

   _____

   _____

   _____

   _____

## *Qualities of an Effective Team Leader*

Before you begin to lead others, it's important that you have a complete picture of the qualities you will be offering the team through your leadership. Do a very basic 360 assessment. Ask people who report to you, your boss, and some of your peers to evaluate your ability to build or rebuild a team. This can help you focus on some of the strengths and work areas before you begin the team-building process.

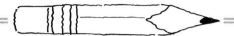

## TEAM LEADERSHIP INVENTORY

Below you will find items related to effective team leadership. Please read each item carefully and choose a number from the scale below to indicate how frequently you use the team leadership behavior described. Then ask 3 to 4 peers, 3 to 5 of your direct reports, and your current supervisor to fill out the inventory and return it to you.

5 = very frequently; 4 = often; 3 = sometimes; 2 = occasionally; 1 = rarely or never

_____ 1. Displays self-awareness

_____ 2. Demonstrates ability to communicate

_____ 3. Listens well

_____ 4. Expresses self well

_____ 5. Manages conflict skillfully

_____ 6. Acts with empathy

_____ 7. Displays ability to develop others

_____ 8. Engages role with self-confidence

_____ 9. Possesses organizational awareness

_____ 10. Acts as a catalyst for change

_____ 11. Maintains optimism

_____ 12. Is adaptable

CONTINUED

13. What do you consider to be my leadership strengths?

_____

_____

_____

14. How would you rate my ability to build a strong team?

_____

_____

_____

15. What suggestions would you have for me in this area?

_____

_____

_____

16. What one piece of advice would you give me as I begin work with a new team?

_____

_____

_____

_____

These are the skills that leaders need for every team-building situation. Although all teams need a leader who has a strong sense of self, how that leader express it may be very different in each group. The new team may be so full of anticipation that the leader will have to both listen to the rapid-fire input and speak well enough to hold the attention of an eager group. The leader who is fixing a problem team needs optimism, organizational awareness, and self-confidence to demonstrate credibility and strength.

The leader of a team that needs to be revitalized requires skills for catalyzing change and energizing the members, as well as heavy doses of motivational expertise. What have you learned about inspiring people? How can you turn a group of "been there—done thats" into spirited champions? The Virtual team requires a leader who has technical skills and exceptional leadership that will keep faceless participants engaged.

For all of these teams, having a title (for example, Senior VP of Marketing) may not be enough. Credibility is more than a title. It's the subtext of the office grapevine that indicates you've done the work, you are to be trusted, and you can deliver.

The leader of teams has to *be* and to *do*. The leader has to *be* many things to many people—a catalyst, a good communicator, and self-confident. They also have a long list of things to *do*. They need to create and inspire a common purpose for all members of the team to rally around. They need to be sure that the right people are on that team by either choosing them or developing the skills to make them good team players. They also need to be certain that the team has the tools and resources to get the goal accomplished. There is nothing more frustrating to a team than to be close to a great accomplishment and then find that the financial support isn't there or the support staff isn't available to help them.

Leaders create an environment for teams by pushing just hard enough to get the work done in a timely manner and providing a sense of play and accomplishment. They also run interference with the rest of the world so the team can concentrate. They make sure that input from the outside is integrated so the team isn't seen as working in isolation. Then, by monitoring progress, the leader ensures that the goal is reached on time and as promised. Team leaders make a promise to deliver: what you promise to do, what you won't take on, who will be part of that promise, how you will do that work, and how you will share that information. It's your charter. It can apply to one project or to a team that works on several projects over time. It is a way of organizing your thoughts and keeping you on track.

In this section, we will concentrate on three of the many leadership tasks: knowing the organization, choosing your team, and identifying the team's purpose.

# Identifying the Team's Purpose

## ORGANIZATIONAL SCAN

Before writing a purpose statement or choosing the team to make it happen, the leader should review the key elements of the organization. This ensures that the work is done in the context of the organization's needs, and not in isolation.

1. Who are we as an organization? What purpose does this organization serve?

   _____

   _____

2. What corporate values guide our work?

   _____

3. What is our corporate responsibility?

   _____

4. What is our vision for the future of the company?

   _____

   _____

5. What is the organization's strategy for achieving that vision?

   _____

   _____

6. What is our brand promise to our customer?

   _____

7. Who are our key customers?

   _____

8. Who is our major competition?

   _____

9. How will our work contribute to the organization's vision for success?

   _____

   _____

# *Purpose Statements*

Every team needs to know exactly what they are expected to do. A strong purpose statement provides continuity and stability. It limits possibility and direction to define the purpose.

It has clear content and is somewhat conservative. The vision comes later and uses the purpose statement as a base from which to soar into the future. Here are some examples of purpose/mission statements from companies you may know.

- ▶ Our purpose is to enable individuals and businesses to manage financial risk. – *American Financial Group*

- ▶ Use our pioneering spirit to responsibly deliver energy to the world. – *Conoco Phillips*

- ▶ To constantly improve what is essential to human progress by mastering science and technology. – *Dow Chemical*

- ▶ To organize the world's information and make it universally accessible and useful. – *Google*

- ▶ To design and sell high performance, super efficient electric cars; to join style, acceleration, and handling with advanced technologies that make them the quickest and the most energy-efficient cars on the planet. – *Tesla Motors*

- ▶ To become the world's first sub-orbital commercial air service provider, reaching an altitude of 62 miles above the earth for a modest 200 thousand dollars per ticket. – *Virgin Galactic*

Before the first team meeting the leader should have a clear sense of the team's purpose and the outcomes required. In defining purpose and outcomes, the leader might ask:

- ▶ What do we do for the organization?

- ▶ What does the team build, create, develop, manage, assess, direct, account for, or protect?

- ▶ What does success look like?

After the team gathers, the leader may want to amend the purpose or clarify it with help from the team.

Not all statements of purpose transform a group of people into a team.

When the VP of sales calls all her managers together and demands a 7% increase in sales and a 10% reduction in travel expenses, there is a very clear message. But will a team achieve those goals or will each manager go back to the office and start working with their own numbers?

One of the most important elements of the purpose statement is that it supports or promotes the organization's strategy and purpose. There needs to be a clear message that this team is playing a critical role in the success of the business.

Take time to review the organization's overall strategy. Then craft a statement that clearly describes the team's purpose as it relates to or promotes that strategy.

Begin by asking these questions:

▶ What are we being asked to do?

▶ What do we want?

▶ What do we most aspire to?

▶ What are our objectives?

▶ What does a desirable outcome look like?

▶ Who are our most important stakeholders?

▶ What are their expectations of our team?

▶ What realities do we have to face?

▶ How does our team's purpose support the purpose and strategy of the organization?

"This is us at our current size."

# ESTABLISHING A TEAM PURPOSE

1. Give each member of the team a blank sheet of paper. Tell them to draw a picture of the "current reality" of the situation your team is trying to remedy or address. Have everyone explain his or her picture to the other team members.

2. Have team members draw a picture of the team that you think "you are called to be." Have everyone explain the picture they have drawn.

3. Make a list of verbs that express the action you hope to take.

   **Examples:** Accomplish, achieve, build, challenge, create, coordinate, deliver, draft, drive, establish, facilitate, generate, implement, innovate, institute, lead, motivate, organize, prepare, provide, reduce, reform, respond, share, supervise, take, teach, translate, validate, and beyond. Use your thesaurus to find just the right words.

   _____

   _____

   _____

4. Discuss common themes, hopes, motivations, expectations and so on.

   _____

   _____

   _____

5. On a blank sheet of paper, draw a collective picture and write the key words or phrases around it.

6. Have someone draft a written version of the team's purpose.

## *A Great Purpose Statement*

▶ Is an image that provides focus and direction for the team's effort

▶ Is short and to the point (10 – 15 words)

▶ Clearly describes what the team is expected to accomplish

▶ Is well-understood by everyone in the team

▶ Emerges from and supports the strategic direction of the organization

▶ Contributes to the long-term purpose of the company

▶ Is clear about what each team member is expected to contribute

▶ Helps each team member understand his/her role

▶ Is do-able

▶ Clearly and specifically describes the need

▶ Is general enough to encourage large thinking

▶ Is specific enough to know where to start

▶ Determines the timeframe

▶ Energizes the people on the team

▶ Improves working relationships because there is a common direction

▶ Pulls people together for the greater good of the organization

### Our Team's Purpose

# Choosing the Best Team

When you are given the rare opportunity to take a new project and you have the basic outline of the task and an approximate timeline, you need to find the people who can create the purpose and make it happen.

Whether choosing a completely new team, revitalizing an old one, or resolving the problems with a troubled team, it is the responsibility of the leader to shape team membership. Making certain that a group of people with many different personal styles, needs, agendas, knowledge, and expertise can come together to accomplish a single goal is an awesome, sometimes overwhelming responsibility. The leader who can pull together a new team has a number of advantages, the central one of which is: You can hand-pick your team members. The abundance of choice can also be overwhelming. The leader who has to live with the team that comes with a new assignment has the challenge of re-constructing a group and making it into a team.

Your first task is to identify the skills and knowledge the members of the group need to meet the challenges of the mission.

## *Jerry Hirschberg's Strategies*

When Jerry Hirschberg was tapped by Nissan to "Build Cars Americans Will Buy," he thought choosing his own new team was a great adventure in itself, and he was quite unconventional in his choices. He concluded that his leadership task was to hire for innovation so his strategies were these:

### Polarity

Hire for opposites, inconsistencies, discontinuities, and ambiguities that ignite the creative spark.

### Unprecedented Thinking

Hire people who expand the limits of what constitutes appropriate, responsible, reliable, and intelligent thought beyond the strictures of the scientific method.

### Beyond the Edges

Hire people for whom creative activity comes to life at the edges by blurring, overlapping, abrading, or breaking through the partitions.

### Synthesis

Synthesis is the impulse to integrate, unify, and bring together. Creativity tolerates and even prefers higher level of disorder and disintegration so it can reorder at newer and higher levels of integration.

Those were the guidelines that Hirschberg used when choosing his unique team. You may think you don't want a team that is quite that undisciplined, constantly questioning, confronting, and stepping over the lines.

But if you hire people with identical backgrounds who are totally compatible, you may discover that all of their ideas sound alike. You may find that instead of an energized, creative team, you are leading a group of nice people who just want to get along together and do things the way they've always been done. Nothing new will come from their work.

## Your Strategies

What are the key guidelines *you* need to consider when choosing or revitalizing your own team?

### Team Purpose

You must begin with a clear and compelling reason for the team's existence. Individuals are motivated by the opportunity to fulfill some larger purpose. If the team members understand what the team is expected to do, they can begin to identify what they will need to do as contributing members.

*What are we expected to do? (Purpose Statement)*

Example: To manage the legal resources of the organization.

### People Needs

If you know the team's purpose and challenge, your next challenge is to decide how to staff the team. What skills, knowledge, and experience are essential for the team's success?

Example: Knowledge of industry law for the organization

Choosing the best team means gathering the right group of people and providing them with an environment in which they can thrive. You can try to choose just the right mix of experience and creativity, styles and attitude, but as the leader it's your task to take those elements and merge them into an extraordinary team. You can get recommendations from others and ask people for résumés and look at files, but the most effective way of establishing a truly great team is to discover the motivations of each team member by talking to them individually. Here are a few of the questions to consider. Following this, you'll find a form you can use for your team.

▶ What are the areas of expertise that will be critical?

▶ What knowledge is essential for this project or task?

▶ What are the personality styles that would be most crucial in accomplishing this mission?

▶ How important is the organizational credibility of this person to this task?

# TEAM CRITERIA CHECKLIST

Use the area below to check off ☑ and describe the characteristics that are most important for your team member selection:

❑ Expertise: _____

_____

❑ Personality: _____

_____

❑ Team qualities: _____

_____

❑ Credibility: _____

_____

❑ Talents: _____

_____

❑ Experience: _____

_____

❑ Education: _____

_____

❑ Variety of thinking styles: _____

_____

❑ Other – please describe: _____

_____

# Part Summary

In this part we examined three critical tasks of a leader:

1. Developing an understanding of the organization

2. Choosing or creating your team

3. Defining the purpose of the team

Assessment tools in this part can help you reflect on and learn from past experiences with leaders and teams you have known. There are also several tools to assess your own capabilities as a leader. As you move up through the organization to more and more responsibilities; you will develop a wider range of leadership skills. One of these assessments can be shared with co-workers, supervisors, and direct reports to give you a 360 review of your abilities. Another evaluation helps to choose team members. Yet another helps create a purpose statement to guide your team as they move through their stages of development.

# Creating the New Team

## *In this part:*

▶ You'll discover ways to get acquainted with a new team.

▶ You'll learn how to lead your new team through the stages of team development.

▶ You'll find an outline for a team charter that will guide your teams.

# If Only It Were This Easy!

You walk into the first meeting of the task force and you can hear the laughter. You see people standing around talking and there is a big screen in front with the organization vision and strategy in big letters. There is also a list of names, including yours.

Jason, who asked you to be in this group, calls the meeting to order with a big smile and says, "Here's the organization strategy for the next three years. You have all been invited here today because I have a great challenge for you. The purpose of our team is to provide the technical support for a project that will take our company to a whole new level. You can see that there is some urgency so let me start by introducing the team I believe can do the job."

Then he introduces each of the 12 team members by name and department and tells the group exactly why each one was chosen—what unique qualities and personality he thinks each can bring to the project and what they will be able to contribute.

You're impressed with the depth and variety of expertise and experience on the team and curious about how you will be introduced. By the time everyone has been acknowledged there is a collective and personal sense of pride. While the project's vision is almost overwhelming in scope and deliverables, there is an excitement in the room and an eagerness to get started.

Jason tells the team there will be plenty of time for getting better acquainted at dinner that evening. You are eager to meet the members of the team because it is obvious they have remarkable skills and knowledge. You wonder how Jason was able to pull together such a team.

Whether creating a new team, repairing a dysfunctional one, or energizing a tired one, a leader needs to be aware of just where along the stages of development the team needs to have help.

When creating a new team, the leader not only gets to choose the team members but also gets to create the environment from the very first day.

The leader who has the task of fixing the problem team needs to do some Re-forming and Constructive Storming before the team can move forward productively.

The leader who is revitalizing an old team needs to step into the Norming stage, where the team is stuck and help them to see the potential they have for excellence.

Finally, the leader for the virtual team gets to Form a new team but also has the challenges of long distance bonding. The following discussion will help you see how to address the needs of the new team and negotiate the stages of their development successfully.

# Stage 1: Forming

Starting with a newly chosen team is a rare and wonderful experience. You will form, storm, norm, and perform. In each stage of development you will introduce new learning to your team. One of the first things Jason did after he chose the members of the team was to spend time getting to know each one. The following is a Getting Acquainted Worksheet for those individual meetings.

## GET ACQUAINTED

Name: _____          Position: _____

**Introduction**: I want to have this conversation so I can better understand how you see this team, how you see me as its leader, and how you see your contributions to the mission of the team.

1. Tell me about yourself. How long have you been with the organization/industry? Why did you choose to come here to work?

2. What successes have you had here? What other career highlights?

3. What do you value about this organization and the people who work here?

4. What do you value about your own work? What expertise/knowledge/experience do you bring to the team?

5. What role do you have (think you can have) in the success of this team?

6. What more would you like to be doing? Is there some talent that's been hidden away or over-looked that we should take advantage of in this new direction we're taking?

7. What's your hope for this team and the work we are hoping to accomplish?

8. How will we know when we're the best?

9. What's your personal plan for the next 30 days to help this team accomplish its goal?

# *The First Meeting: Leadership Tasks*

At the first meeting, as leader you should:

- ▶ Introduce the team.
- ▶ Define the vision.
- ▶ Define the purpose.
- ▶ Hand out assignments.

## Introducing the Team

When the leader finishes speaking with each team member, it's time to hold the first meeting and share insights about the potential in the group. The leader should introduce everyone and share the name, title, work history, and some unique strength each person brings to the task. This does several things for the team:

- ▶ Puts each team member in the spotlight and shares information the team member may not think to share.

- ▶ Gives everyone equal time and helps focus the team on why each was chosen or what their leader considers to be the value they bring to the team.

- ▶ Lets everyone know what the leader's expectations are of each team member.

- ▶ Lets everyone know what type of culture the leader is imagining.

## Defining Vision and Strategy

You must provide an overview of the organization's vision and strategy.

## Defining the Team's Purpose

Identify the team's purpose and give a brief overview of what this team is expected to contribute to the vision and strategy of the larger organization.

## Assignments

The leader may also want to hand out the following assignments:

- ▶ A personality assessment for further team understanding

- ▶ A worksheet with the team's purpose statement

- ▶ An organizational scan to help team members gain a common understanding of what is important to the organization's future and how their assignment can contribute to its success

# Stage 2: Constructive Storming

Once the group has had time to consider what they are being asked to do and who they have to work with to do it, the Storming stage can become confrontational. Group members may jockey for position, challenge the leader, and question their roles and the team's purpose. It may begin as soon as the second meeting.

The leader who understands the dangers of Storming stage can minimize its negative effects. Do this by educating the team during the Forming stage about the positive use of Storming. It should be used to express divergent perspectives, clarify personal roles, and identify a variety of hidden skills. and divide up the work in unusual, creative ways. Anticipate some Storming behavior and call it out. (Identify it when it's happening.) Let the group know that they have a very short time to get the Storm out of their system before they need to move on.

If you have promoted a collaborative culture in the Forming stage, you can expect a lot of debate in the Storming stage. It should be done with an eye toward growth and development of the team and best outcome for the common purpose. Team members will be eager to question and pursue the best answers together. Some leaders think if they don't mention this stage it won't happen. But it's better to talk about it, name it, make it a learning experience, and move on.

# STORMING DISCUSSION

1.  What concerns do you have about what we are being asked to do?

    _____

    _____

2.  What concerns do you have about the role you are asked to play on this team?

    _____

    _____

3.  What's the best team you were ever on?

    _____

    _____

4.  Why? What made them so great?

    _____

    _____

5.  What can we take away from their experience?

    _____

    _____

6.  What is each one here willing to do to use this stage positively and move on quickly?

    _____

    _____

**"** *The peak efficiency of knowledge and strategy is to make conflict unnecessary."*

**–Sun Tzu, *The Art of War***

## *Positive Storming Tools*

Consistent with Sun Tzu's quote, we believe that a good leader anticipates the need to sort out roles and establish guidelines. The leader should encourage constructive disagreement in the name of excellence. We also believe much destructive conflict can be avoided with good planning, good tools, and good leadership. Here are some ideas to help the leader anticipate and lead the team through this necessary stage of team development.

Before there is a Storm about who does what, engage the team in a role clarification exercise. Here are some thoughts to get you started:

1. Provide poster board, markers, and space to post the team's work for all to see. This common visual record keeps everyone on the same page in the discussion as it unfolds, and with the elements of the decisions that you make.

2. Introduce the exercise by briefly explaining four aspects of a role:

   ▷ **Conception:** What I believe this role should be.

   ▷ **Expectation:** What I believe others expect of me in this role.

   ▷ **Acceptance:** What I am willing to do in this role.

   ▷ **Behavior:** What I actually do; how I spend my time; what my priorities are in this role.

3. Give the group 20 minutes to record their thoughts about these aspects of their role on the team. Have each person share their thoughts and entertain questions.

**Outcome:** Each person on the team should go away from the meeting with a clear understanding of their contribution to the team and the purpose of their role.

# Stage 3: Norming

They named themselves "The Posse" because they were well-armed (with knowledge and experience) to seek out and contain the bad guys and to provide safety and economic success for the stakeholders. The leader was charismatic and driven and she chose team members for their ability to make things happen, to be creative, and to enjoy each other's idiosyncrasies. She protected them from some of upper management's conservative business strategy confinements and encouraged them to imagine an exciting future and to design the plans for getting there. She found money for experimentation, provided education and coaching, and made sure that team members were given opportunities to bring their ideas before senior leadership on a regular and frequent basis. Long after team members moved on to other departments, locations, or companies, they continued their connections. Within the company, the team's charter—their promise to deliver— was legendary.

There is more that goes into delivering on your purpose statement than just getting a group together to come up with some good idea and then handing it over to another group to implement. By agreeing to lead or be a part of a team, you have made a promise to the organization that has many parts to it. A charter is the team's promise to deliver and to do so in a particular manner.

The team charter outlines who is on the team, what the purpose is, what they will and won't do, how they will work together toward their goal, and their timeframe. The charter describes the culture they want to create. It is the team's promise to deliver and it is the leader's framework for creating the most successful team environment.

If your team has had a positive Storming stage during which they celebrated their differences in roles, expectations, and skills rather than arguing about them, you've already begun the Norming stage of your team's development. Norming is a time for settling into the culture and getting the work started.

> *"Coming together is a beginning. Keeping together is progress. Working together is success."*
>
> **–Henry Ford**

## *Charter: Our Promise to Deliver*

| Decision Area | Definition of What's Needed |
|---|---|
| **Team Name:** | Who are we? |
| **Purpose:** | What is our purpose? <br> Why does the team exist? |
| **Scope of Work:** | What will we deliver to our stakeholders? <br> Will we improve, develop, test, or implement processes, identify issues, establish priorities, or remove barriers? |
| **Not to Be Addressed:** | What work won't we take on? <br> What are the boundaries that define the team's work? |
| **Team Values:** | What values/rules guide our interactions? |
| **Code of Conduct:** | What behaviors can we expect from ourselves and others? |
| **Roles:** | What are the responsibilities of each group member? |
| **Timeframes:** | How much time will be needed to complete our task? <br> When and how often should we? |
| **Format:** | How will we conduct the meetings? |
| **Leader:** | Who is responsible for bringing the team together, leading actions, and attending to the logistics of the group? <br> Who is in charge? |
| **Process Owner:** | Who is supporting this team at the executive level? |
| **Team Members:** | Who should be a part of the group? |
| **Membership Criteria:** | What qualifies as membership of the group? <br> What are the contributions of each member? |
| **Facilitators:** | Do we need an outside facilitator? |
| **Stakeholders:** | Who is affected by the group's decisions and actions? |
| **Communication Plan:** | Who needs to know about the work of the group? <br> What do they need to know, and how often? |
| **Language:** | What working definitions or common language are needed? |
| **Evaluation Criteria:** | How do we measure effectiveness of the group this month? This quarter? This year? |

At a minimum the team's charter should include the following:

▶ Name

▶ Purpose and scope

▶ How progress will be tracked

▶ Values

## Name of the Team

If the team is going to be together for any length of time (3–4 months or more), naming it can just make it easier to keep track of for meetings and membership. But if you're going to be together for a long time, find a name that unites the team. Find the most interesting way to be identified. This can be a strong bonding tool.

## Purpose and Scope of Work

The purpose statement is your promise to deliver. It should be strong enough in word and tone to inspire the group and short enough to remember easily. Once you have written a clear purpose, the scope of work defines the work more specifically. It's also important to outline what you will *not* do. There have to be some boundaries or the team will be together forever as they keep finding more and more to add on to their task. There needs to be a place (call it the Parking Lot) to record these ideas so they don't get lost, but leave them and form another team later for those great ideas.

## Tracking Progress

As the team moves toward its goal, tracking progress is critical to the team's success. Keep the purpose front and center at all stages of the team's work.

▶ Are we still on track with our goal?

▶ What did we accomplish at this meeting toward our goal?

▶ Is work being finished?

▶ Is the team still intact and viable?

▶ Is there still a sense of focus?

▶ Does our direction still make sense?

▶ Are we missing something we didn't anticipate at the beginning?

▶ Do we see an end in sight?

▶ How are team members doing with their assignments?

## Team Values

Teams need to agree ahead of time on values that will guide their behavior. Ask yourselves these questions:

▶ How will we work together?

▶ What are three or four values we can agree on to help us monitor our behaviors as a team?

You may choose to review your organizational values and use those but it's worth the time to discuss the specific values this team will abide by for their working relationships and to have them displayed or reviewed periodically.

> *Respect your fellow human being, treat them fairly, disagree with them honestly, enjoy their friendship, explore your thoughts about one another candidly, work together for a common goal and help one another achieve it."*

> **–Bill Bradley**

# TEAM VALUES

**Instructions:** Copy the values on the next page onto card stock, cut them out, and have the team put the values into three piles:

1. Those that are absolutely necessary for this team

2. Those that are good but not essential

3. Those that are least important to the team

Then choose three words that will guide the work of the team.

1. _____

2. _____

3. _____

# VALUES CARDS

| | | | | |
|---|---|---|---|---|
| Achievement | Caring | Caution | Challenge | Communication |
| Competition | Cooperation | Creativity | Curiosity | Customer focus |
| Determination | Diversity | Fairness | Fun | Flexibility |
| Freedom | Passion | Growth | Honesty | Relationships |
| Competency | Consensus | Perseverance | Recognition | Tolerance |
| Individualism | Innovation | Involvement | Learning | Organization |
| Productivity | Profitability | Quality | Quantity | Respect |
| Responsibility | Risk | Security | Service to others | Speed |
| Task focus | Teamwork | Uniqueness | Winning | Urgency |
| Trust | Loyalty | Humility | Integrity | |

## Roles

At the Forming stage of team development it was enough for the leader to identify the roles that each team member is expected to fill for the group.

"Cathy will keep us in line with HR policies as we move forward. Josh is our engineering expert and will lead during the design phase. And we'll defer to Dora's expertise in process improvement. As the leader of this team, I am just here to see that we use everyone's expertise and we finish a great project on time."

There are roles that are determined by education and expertise. Some emerge due to personality types. At this stage of team development, these types may be just be hinted at. Rather than wait until they are full-blown nuisances, you may want to discuss some common team roles. You can ask people to serve in some of these roles as a way of bringing humor into the group process and as a way of calling attention to it later when the group sees the behavior in one of its members.

"Bill, do you want to take over the role of 'Devil's Advocate' in this discussion? You have been asking some hard questions that we should consider. You can have that role today. What questions are on your mind? What are we missing?"

At the Norming stage you may want to review those initial role assignments to ensure that they are still valid.

## Timeframe

Let team members understand the time commitment they will be asked to make. Will this take them away from their "real" jobs 10% of the time or 20% for the next six months? What is the project deadline? How much time will be required to make that deadline? At this stage you may have to make some adjustments on time requirements as you get further into the real work of the team.

## Format

Team members need a consistent and useful meeting format. Do you start every meeting with updates or progress or a check-in or agenda items? Do you assign time limits to discussions? More importantly, do you lay out a format and then stick with it—or go wherever and never finish agenda items? How do you prioritize agenda items and time?

These are all questions for the first meeting. It will be harder to discuss these if you wait until there's an issue.

- ▶ Meeting dates
- ▶ Meeting times
- ▶ Check-in/Progress review
- ▶ Agenda items
- ▶ Project completion date

## Process Owner

Who has the final say on your common purpose? Who can support your team if it comes up with an unusual request or radical decision about the outcome? That person needs to make an appearance at one of the first meetings to set the tone and to offer advice and support as you get closer to your goals.

## Team Members — Who Is In and Who Is Out?

Especially if the group is high profile, there may be a rush to join the team. If the organization has trust concerns, everyone may want to be on the team to ensure that his or her perspective is present and needs are met. How large a group will it take to connect with key decision makers in the organization and yet be small enough to get something accomplished? In the Norming stage, you may discover that while the original team size was perfect at the beginning, you now need to bring people with specific expertise into the group for short periods of time.

## Facilitators

It is very helpful to have someone other than the leader paying attention to the process while the leader pays attention to the content of the meetings. Facilitators can summarize, ask process kinds of questions, make observations about team member participation, and review leadership skills before and after the meetings. Consider using a facilitator when you feel you need another set of eyes to pick up on all the team dynamics.

## Primary Stakeholders

Who will be most affected by the work of this group? How can you gather feedback and gain their support? How can you let them know you will be putting their interests forward in the discussions and do all of this without having to include them in every meeting?

## Communication Plan

Who needs to know what you're doing? How often do they need to hear from you? How much detail is important to keep the key stakeholders up to date?

## Language

At one recent meeting that included some fairly new hires, one of the other participants thoughtfully handed out the "Corporate Dictionary" with all the acronyms and industry lingo that was very helpful to everyone. What words need to be defined before the meeting? How can the leader point out words that aren't common language throughout the process so everyone has the same level of understanding?

## Criteria for Evaluation

What does success look like? How will you know you've achieved it? What is the measure—not just numbers and not just a plan? Results are important, but so is a measure of how well the team performed while achieving them.

In the Norming phase, the group becomes a tribe with its own language, rules, values, roles, in-jokes, and mission, and even a tribal name and motto. They may even respond as a whole to criticism or input from outsiders. That doesn't mean there isn't conflict, but the ways to deal with it are known and practiced by all (most of the time!). Getting to that place requires coaching and education by the team leader and others.

"Hal, this team needs a guy with special skills like yours."

# Stage 4: Performing

Everything the team said they would deliver is being delivered—and on time!

The Performing stage doesn't necessarily mean that there are no more conflicts, but it does mean that the major issues have been resolved and the mission's conclusion is in sight. This stage can be very exciting and there is a strong sense of urgency to deliver on the promise.

The team has figured out who they are in the Forming stage. They've explored all the differences they have in the Storming stage and followed all the rules in the Norming stage. Now it's all coming together in this Performing stage. In this stage, the team is clear about who is doing what, and how things need to be done. The norms that were chosen earlier have been actualized, and the group is functioning within its agreements to one another. All of the planning and negotiating is now paying off in terms of productive work.

There is a real sense of accomplishment and satisfaction as the results that were targeted and desired are now showing up as very real products of the team's efforts.

# Stage 5: Adjourning

Tuckman's stages of team development originally ended at Performing because once you have produced the desired outcome, what else is there? But he later acknowledged another stage. Many teams don't realize that it is an essential stage: Adjourning.

It is a time for the team to disengage. They need to say good-bye, pack up their notes, and move on to the next adventure. Some teams go out to celebrate or a member of the executive team comes to thank them for their service. But the organization misses a great opportunity for learning if that's all there is. The Adjourning stage can be use to articulate and record the lessons learned from the team's work and the changes their work delivered to the organization. They call them debriefings or downloads.

Gather the team for one last work session. Invite their supervisors, the process owner, and other interested people. Ask these questions and record the answers.

1. What did we accomplish? For the organization? For ourselves?

2. What did we learn about ourselves and our ability to work together as a team?

3. What did we like most about our assignment? Least?

4. What do we consider to be the greatest successes for this project?

5. What did we learn about the organization and its support of teamwork?

6. What changes do we think there have been in the organization because of the work of our team?

7. What more could we do?

8. What are the next steps we think the organization may want to take?

9. What was the one thing each of us gained by being part of this team?

As the leader, you should then summarize the work and offer to send copies of the notes from the meeting so others can benefit from the experience. Then, thank the team and adjourn.

# Part Summary

For the leader, creating a whole new team and being responsible for a specific contribution to the success of the organization is both terrifying and exhilarating. With the tools provided in this section, the leader can anticipate possible problems and turn them into learning experiences. The Get Acquainted interview and First Meeting section can help the leader set the stage for team expectations. The Storming stage can be turned into a constructive step in the team's development with education about ways to use it in a positive manner. The charter is a guide that can help the leader stay on track with values clarification, reminders about communication, process owner involvement, team purpose, and role clarification. One of the outcomes from the work of this team may very well be that as the team members move onto other teams, they will remember and describe *this team* as *the most memorable, most productive, and best team experience.*

# Fixing the Problem Team

*Teamwork is essential—it allows you to blame someone else. "*

–Unknown

*In this part:*

▶ How to begin the process of Re-Forming a problem team

▶ Using Constructive Storming with a problem team

▶ The Norming and Performing stages when fixing a problem team

# Re-Forming a Problem Team

It's inevitable! "Who are we?" is the first question on the team charter. In a new team, you already know a lot about who they are. But we don't all get to start fresh and hand-pick people for a team. Often we are assigned a team and sometimes it doesn't come close to the ideal. As the team leader you are responsible for building a great team out of whatever you've been given. If you have come into the kind of Storming team that gives this stage its name, you can expect hostility and lack of collaboration or progress toward the goal. Your ability to lead will be tested. There will be conflicting ideas about how to get to the Performing stage.

At his first meeting, Todd realized his promotion to head of sales may not have been such a reward. Some new sales reps were late to arrive and weren't concerned about it. When he asked for agenda items, no one had anything to add. There were many messages via body language—sighing, eye rolling, and side conversations. When one rep stood and announced he needed to leave early, Todd ended the meeting.

*That meeting was just the most public indication of the team's problem.*

People stopped in Todd's office all week with minor complaints about a co-worker or a system issue. When Todd asked for specific information no one had clear answers. After the first week, managers from other departments asking Todd how he was "surviving the team from _____."

*Where do you start to fix a team that has so many problems?*

This wasn't a problem of Todd's making and he didn't choose the characters in this drama. But now they were all his. It is tempting to begin the very next day by imposing some structure on the group.

## Memo

**From**: Todd

**To**: Sales Team

Starting this week:

1. Everyone will be at the weekly meetings on time.

2. No one will leave early without speaking to me first.

3. Agenda items have to be in to me 24 hours before the meeting.

4. All administrative work has to be signed by me.

5. If you don't have an excuse, I expect you to be at the full meeting.

Todd began to feel like a first grade teacher. And the team's reaction? "He's treating us like children!" "No problem, we'll crack this guy in no time."

# Re-Forming the Problem Team

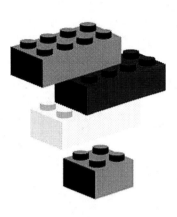

When a group spends time in the Storming stage, there are many hidden filters that impede team progress. They might be lessons learned from educational backgrounds that are no longer valid in the workplace. They may be organizational paradigms or theories of how the organization should work that prevent team members from seeing other ways of working. Some bring cultural norms to work and impose them on interactions with others. Even more powerful are the values and beliefs developed since childhood. These lessons learned from childhood, education, and culture become behaviors in the workplace. If one's belief is that those in charge know best, one is not likely to challenge directives. Someone who believes that win/lose is the way corporate America stays ahead in the world may approach every interaction as a competition.

If a group is already entrenched in the Storming stage, it is helpful to go back to stage 1 and do some "Re-Forming" to help the group get past some of these beliefs. But before you start adding to the groups' list of rules, consider doing a diagnosis of the group. The format and the tone of the diagnosis are critical. The questions you ask and how you ask them will set the tone for months or years to come.

There are two approaches to diagnosis:

▶ Problem identification

▶ Identification of the successes and potential

## Problem Identification Approach

Some people like this approach because it feels like they're getting to bottom of things. There are problems, and they are 1, 2, and 3. If we fix these, we'll be fine. Except everyone knows that isn't exactly how it works, so the answers are incomplete. And they tend to be negative—you asked about the problems!

"Tell me what you see as the three major issues we need to fix here."

"Tell me what you think we should fix first."

"Where are the major problems that I will need to address?"

A leader probably won't need to ask much more because it is so easy for people to get into a problem identification mindset. One complaint leads to the next. It can be a very demoralizing conversation. There are rarely solutions to follow the list of problems. It may seem overwhelming to imagine positive outcomes. Even if there were suggestions for how to solve these problems, the team has not learned how to work together to find those solutions.

## Identifying the Success

*There is a better way*. It may be with a Storming team that there is no reason to talk with people about successes and strengths of the group. What good could come from such pessimistic attitudes? Questions that focus on the positive may be suspect with this group so it is better to ask the questions during private conversations with individuals. Before you begin:

1.  Provide for the safety of the group members. They may not be comfortable with this approach or with the idea of sharing thoughts and feelings about the group.

2.  Be specific about how this information is to be used—to improve the culture and successfully deliver on the vision.

3.  Give collective feedback and act on what you hear. If you gather the information and no one sees any improvements, they will be even less interested in sharing with you the next time.

# TEAM RE-FORMING INTERVIEW GUIDE

## Introduction

I wanted to get to know each person in the department, so I thought I'd do some interviews. I plan to record your responses but I will share only summaries of all the interviews I do with the whole team.

1. Tell me why you came to work here.

2. How long have you worked in this department/unit/team?

3. What have been some of the successes of the team?

4. What do you see as the strengths of the team?

5. What do you like best about this team?

6. What is the most exciting work you have done here?

7. What do you see as the potential of this team?

8. What are the areas that could be improved?

9. What challenges do you see for the team?

10. What things make you effective as team members?

11. What holds you back from being as effective as you would like?

12. What could we do to make sure the roles and responsibilities of team members are clear and well structured?

13. What particular team skills would you like to learn more about?

14. Who are the positive influences on the team?

15. Who contributes most to the success of the team?

16. What do you value about the people who work with you?

17. What are some things we could do to make this team more productive? More fun?

# TEAM MEMBER SELF-REVIEW

Rate yourself on the following characteristics of a successful team player, using a 1 to 5 scale as follows:

1 = Low    5 = High

_____ 1. **Technical competence**: contributes to the team's needs

_____ 2. **Results orientation**: has drive, hustle, appropriate aggressiveness

_____ 3. **Commitment**: is focused on the success of the team

_____ 4. **Flexibility**: is adaptable and willing to adjust

_____ 5. **Communication**: is open, direct, and sensitive for the good of individuals and the team

_____ 6. **Process awareness**: is able to watch from a distance and be objective

### Feedback from Interviews and Self-Reviews

When you look for strengths and successes, you'll discover many things the team should feel good about. The more you pursue this approach the more the team will sense pride in work already done and ignite energy for what's to come.

As soon as you have done the interviews it is important to share your findings with the team, without attributing remarks to any one person. Do an overview of the successes you recorded. Be specific about the steps you intend to take that are based on the successes of the past. Let them know how much you learned and what you intend to do with the feedback. This discussion will set the stage for the work that needs to be done and the approach you will use to get it done.

## Re-Forming Leader Strategies

With a team that is struggling and well into a Storming mode, you may want to go back to the Forming fundamentals before you address the more difficult Storming concerns.

Here are several points to consider:

### Give the team the feedback from the interviews.

Use that as a basis for generating enthusiasm for the team approach.

### Start meetings on time.

If you wait for latecomers, you reward their behavior and send the message that it's acceptable to be late.

### Clarify the length of the meeting at the beginning.

Ensure that everyone is "on board" with the stopping time and then end it on time. This makes it more difficult for individuals to leave early and allows you and the group to make adjustments up front if someone is planning an early departure. If early departures become a regular occurrence, make that "norm" a topic for team discussion and decision making. Ask for new commitments and hold one another to agreements.

### Make Sure All Views Are Heard

If a participants won't let go of their viewpoints, hear them out, record the viewpoints on the flip chart to validate them, and ask directly if there is anything else they need before they can let go of them and allow the team to move on.

### Call on Participants Directly

Or physically move close to them if they are doing something else (writing a memo, and so on). If this doesn't get them back with you, speak to them afterwards or during a break.

### Touch Base with People Who Demonstrate Dramatic Nonverbals

"I see you're shaking your head.... Do you have a different approach you'd like to suggest?" The participant may not have been aware of the head-shaking, and may strive to control the body language. If the participant's behavior continues and becomes disruptive or extremely annoying, wait until a break and share your observations. "Every time you shake your head, you interrupt the meeting. Is there something bothering you?"

### Agree on Not Evaluating Ideas for a Set Period

To deal with negative participants, ask the team to agree to a process of not evaluating ideas for a set period of time; then use this agreement to address anyone who violates it.

### Move Close to Limit Side Conversations

If a side conversation begins or there is a perpetual whisperer, move close to them and they will usually stop. Ask people to maintain their focus on the project or discussion at hand. If necessary confront the group or individual's tendency to start side conversations and directly (and constructively) share your frustration with side conversations. Ask them to stick with the team's focus.

### Move Close to Overly Verbal People

The most subtle technique for dealing with an overly verbal person involves your physical position in relation to them. Try moving closer to them while they are talking and maintain eye contact until you are standing right in front of them. Then, shift your focus and call on someone else. You may have to deal with verbose people outside the meeting. You can also ask them to be the "recorder." They (recorders) don't talk, they just write down what's said. If nothing else works, you may have to confront them directly.

### Address Gossip Directly

"Do you know that for a fact?"; "Are you sure?"; "Can anyone else verify that?"; "How could we find out the answer to that question? Who would know?" When in doubt, defer the issue until the truth can be obtained.

### Call a Halt to Verbal Intimidation

Validate the right of participants to disagree with one another, but redirect them to constructive negotiation rather than power or threats. If necessary, call a break and meet with the "intimidator." Ask for his/her support in putting the discussion on hold until it can be dealt with constructively.

### Call on Nonparticipants by Name

Ask for their views or opinion.

# Constructive Storming

The problem team probably had a brief moment of success when they originally formed, but when they got to the Storm stage they got stuck there. The members of the team never agreed on a code of conduct. They made rules for individuals, not the team. They argued about division of labor, tasks, and roles. There was in-fighting which made it impossible to get to the Norming stage. There are several problems to address before they can move on. One of those is the belief in the concept of win-lose: Someone else has to lose before I can win, because there's no way we can both be winners.

## *Win-Lose vs. Win-Win*

A key theme in management development and team building is the concept of "Win-Win." This behavior promotes collaboration and cooperation, but is an unknown concept in a team that has gotten stuck in the Storming stage. They are much more likely to embrace the concept of win-lose.

### Win-Lose

*One party gains at the other's expense.*

A win-lose situation is often a result of inappropriate competition and often relies on power to carry it through (for example, position power, physical power, relationship power, and so on). The concept of win-lose is said to come from a position of "scarcity"—that is, there is only so much of a given thing and I had better make sure I get mine even if it is at your expense.

### Win-Win

*Both parties gain from a solution.*

This is based on the idea that if we can truly collaborate, there is always the possibility that we aren't limited to simply finding a way to divide up the pie, and we may be able to create more pie. The result will be that both (or all) parties can get what they want or need.

The following are some suggestions for moving a team from Stuck Storming to Constructive Storming:

▶ Clearly identify win-win as a team value.

▶ Adopt and teach effective problem-solving and decision-making processes.

▶ Reward cooperation and collaboration.

### Clearly Identify Win-Win Dealings as a Team Value

Team leaders need to be clear that they will work with team members and others from a win-win perspective. Long-term trust and relationships depend on it. Of course, leaders must not only state that win-win is a value, they also must model it in their day-to-day dealings. This is one place where "Don't do as I do…do as I say" simply does not work.

We live in a country that valued fierce individualism for generations. Our political and social system is rich with examples of how to climb the ladder and get yours no matter who you have to walk on.

Our traditional corporate model has also not been a great example of—or training ground for—teamwork and collaboration. We must teach these skills and ensure that they stick. We need collaboration skills in the most difficult of situations and that is exactly the time when we naturally fall back into old habits—unless there is ample support and training for doing it a different way.

### Adopt and Teach Common Problem-Solving and Decision-Making Processes

When win-lose has the chance to thrive, those who can't compete are tempted to adopt "covert strategies" to level the playing field and gain the opportunity to win. Likewise, those who are skilled may be tempted to use their superior skills in a shady manner. If no rules govern play, the game often goes to the best "jungle fighters." But there is access to and training in a common approach to problem-solving, then each member has a road map to allow their full participation and contribution.

### Reward Cooperation and Collaboration

The organization's recognition, reward, and compensation systems should be retooled to ensure they support and encourage teamwork, collaboration, and fair play. Many (feeble) attempts to develop quality systems, self-directed teams, and other participatory work processes are doomed because the old reward systems remain intact and work against change. This is an example of a win-lose system.

# *Dealing with Win-Lose Situations as They Arise*

Here are some down-and-dirty tools for avoiding win-lose situations:

▶ Focus (or refocus) on the group's purpose, vision, and/or objectives.

▶ Give all parties an opportunity to have a voice and to be heard.

▶ Avoid individual (or group) tendencies to jump to solutions prematurely.

▶ Confront attempts to circumvent the process.

▶ Don't recognize, reward, or promote people or actions that result in win-lose outcomes.

### Focus on Purpose

If the group is locked in discussion of a few closely held opinions and several of the members are heavily invested in their own solutions, you are headed for a win-lose outcome. Acknowledge the solutions on the table and remind the team there may be other alternatives that haven't been explored. Restate the purpose of the group and its vision for working together. Restate the objectives and ask the team to engage in generating more alternatives. This often helps to depersonalize the discussion and present additional alternatives that may not have been available previously.

### Give All Parties a Voice

Many win-lose processes boil down to attempts to remove others from the process or to allow only select (often highly biased) portions of their needs and positions. Open up the process to provide the opportunity to use the best the team can offer.

### Don't Jump to Solutions Prematurely

Sometimes the rush to a solution is an intentional ploy to prevent alternatives from coming to light, but frequently the desire to get the problem solved and to get on with it will lead a group to jump on the first solution that appears to cover the need.

### Confront Attempts to Circumvent the Process

If some value the process but others do not, the team will quickly become cynical about the stated value and will see that "some are more equal than others." Those in positions of power must be held to win-win processes if the rest of the team is to believe that they are true values.

### Don't Reward Behaviors That Lead to Win-Lose Outcomes

Jack Welch of General Electric Corporation made a powerful commitment to his shareholders and a powerful statement to management and employees when he stated in the shareholders annual report that the organization could no longer afford managers who are able to get results "on the backs of the employees." He made it clear that GE would help those managers find opportunities elsewhere because those kinds of management tactics are not consistent with the values of General Electric. This is a powerful statement against win-lose management.

# Confrontation

The term "confrontation" has an ugly implication. But you need to confront any team member or co-worker who is constantly irritating and resists change. Confrontation brings up strong feelings of fear, anger, frustration, worry, and many thoughts about why you shouldn't even bother. Begin by looking at those fears.

- ▶ I don't want to ruin the relationship.
- ▶ I might lose control.
- ▶ I don't know how to confront.
- ▶ What if he or she starts crying?
- ▶ What if the other person starts yelling at me?
- ▶ What if he or she quits?
- ▶ What if they go to my boss or to human resources?

These are all worst-case possibilities. However, if you handle confrontation skillfully and follow a few guidelines for dealing with people, it's possible the relationship will become stronger and more durable afterward.

## Dealing with Differences

First of all, *remember that confrontation is nothing more than dealing directly with your differences*. So deal with your differences as constructively as possible:

- ▶ Be direct and to the point. State your problem without camouflaging it.
- ▶ Be specific. Give examples and talk about behavior, not motives.
- ▶ Maintain a constructive tone. Describe what happened and how it was different from what you expected or desired.
- ▶ Describe the consequences of the person's behavior.
- ▶ Tell them what you would like them to do instead.
- ▶ Listen to their point of view.
- ▶ Don't blame or name call.
- ▶ Don't get off onto another subject.
- ▶ Offer to help.
- ▶ Own your piece of the problem.

# CONFRONTATION GUIDE

**I have a problem…**

**When you** (describe the problem behavior): _____

_____

_____

**I feel** (describe your feeling response): _____

_____

_____

**I would rather you** (describe preferred behavior): _____

_____

_____

**If you do** (describe positive result): _____

_____

_____

**If you don't** (describe consequences): _____

_____

_____

**Note:** The consequence is simply a description of what you perceive to be the negative results that will occur if the requested change doesn't occur. It should not be a threat of punishment or retribution.

Use the suggested structure as a framework for thinking about how to constructively engage with the other person. Don't use it as a script—you may find that the other party does not know his or her "part."

> *What we need to do is learn to work in the system, by which I mean that everybody, every team, every platform, every division, every component is there not for individual competitive profit or recognition, but for contribution to the system as a whole on a win-win basis."*
>
> **–W. Edward Deming**

## *Moving Misfits to a Better Fit*

Not everyone can be part of every team. The Storming stage brings that to the forefront very quickly. It's a time of testing, questioning, and pushing. It is also a time for building trust and connections. Some people are not comfortable in that environment. Even when the leader follows all the best leadership practices, there will be times when a member of the team has to be un-invited.

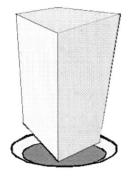

That's not an easy task; especially if the person is there because he/she has essential expertise or has been there for a long time.

Begin by having a private conversation. You can share your observations that he/she has not seemed engaged in the way you had hoped. The following are some points for discussion that can lead you both to the conclusion that the work of this team is not the best use of his/her time and energy or that this team member will need to step up to continue with the team or find a better use of skills.

- ▶ How do you think the team is progressing toward its goal?
- ▶ Is the team using your expertise the way you'd hoped?
- ▶ What more could you be doing for this team? What are we missing?
- ▶ Are we going in a direction that requires your input at this time?
- ▶ Do you feel comfortable with the way we are using your talents?
- ▶ How do you think you can be the most help to the team or to the rest of the organization right now?
- ▶ Do you want to continue to work with this team or is there work you feel you should be doing?

At this point, the team member may see that he/she wants to continue to work with the team and has a lot to contribute. This is the time to share more of your observations about attitude, behavior, or level of interaction. Then you can elicit suggestions about how to change those perceptions and behaviors to be better engaged with the team. It may also be helpful to review the values, common purpose, and membership criteria from the charter.

# Norming and Performing

### Getting the Problem Team Ready for Norming

After Re-Forming and Constructively Re-Storming a Problem team, you are ready to continue with the Norming stage. Look at the charter again and review any points the team may need to reconsider and modify.

### Performing with the Problem Team

At this point, the Problem team is well on its way to delivering on the promise of their vision. They are working well together and you are ready to take on another challenge.

# Part Summary

If you an especially high-potential leader in an organization, you can expect that someone will give you the opportunity to take on a problem team to see just how skillful you can be. Problem teams often take pride in their image of being difficult. They may be under the illusion that their behavior makes them stars. They may get their way with other departments who are just tired of dealing with them. They may have moments of great success. But you can help them review those successes of the past to find ways to duplicate them in a sustainable manner. Your greatest challenge is to redirect the storming stage into open, direct, productive interactions. This part gives you a model for setting guidelines that will get the problem team back on track. And for those team members who need just a little extra convincing, there is also a confrontation guide.

# Revitalizing the Inactive Team & Creating the Virtual Team

❝ *Wild ducks make a lot of noise, but they also have the sense to benefit from occasionally flying in formation.* ❞

**–Unknown**

## *In this part:*

▶ Revitalizing an inactive team by re-focusing on vision

▶ The stages of team development for virtual teams

▶ The intact team

▶ Tips for building a high-performance team

# Revitalizing the Inactive Team

―――― CASE STUDY: West Wind Clinic ――――

The West Wind Clinic was in serious danger of losing patients to the new University clinic that was being planned. West Wind had never anticipated any competition and hadn't bothered to recruit patients or provide new, innovative services. Now this inactive team needs to be rejuvenated, reenergized, and resuscitated. They are so out of touch, they may be in danger of being bypassed by their competitors or even losing their business. They ambled through their Forming, Storming, and Norming stages years before. Some of the rules have been adapted over time. Communication has evolved into shortcuts. If you went down the charter list, they'd say they have it covered. Their purpose is now as it was 12 years ago—"To bring good health care to the community." The values they picked back then at a team meeting are posted on every door. Nurses, technicians, and physicians all know their roles and responsibilities, though that has changed a little over time with new technology and the addition of physician's assistants. They even do both internal and external evaluations to ensure that they are doing a good job among themselves and for their patients.

An inactive team gets stuck at the Norming stage. They are doing a lot that is right but can't seem to move ahead to the stage where they can create and deliver a new vision. To survive, their task is to generate excitement in the future and revisit their long-range plans, to set new goals, and to get moving.

## *Rewriting the Vision*

> " *I believe that this nation should commit itself to achieving the goal, before this decade is out, of landing a man on the moon and returning him safely to the Earth.*"

**–President John F. Kennedy, May 25, 1961**

Despite skeptics who thought it could not be done, Kennedy's dream became a reality when Neil Armstrong and Buzz Aldrin left dusty footprints on the moon. Nothing unites a group faster than an outrageous mandate. The President's challenge to NASA to put a man on the moon by the year 1971 was a very clear directive. Every person in the agency knew exactly what his or her focus would be and how to contribute to a goal of that magnitude.

And so on July 20, 1969, two years before the goal, Neil Armstrong stepped onto the lunar surface—"One small step for man, one giant leap for mankind."

> **But this is not merely a race. Space is open to us now; and our eagerness to share its meaning is not governed by the efforts of others. We go into space because whatever mankind must undertake, free men must fully share."**
>
> **–John F. Kennedy**

Kennedy's vision guided NASA's human space flight program from the beginning. Mercury, Gemini, and Apollo missions were designed with his objective in mind.

An effective team has a common image of the ideal result of the team's work. Like blueprints for a building, the team's vision guides members on the appropriate steps to pursue their vision. More than a blueprint, however, the team's vision is steeped in closely held values and ideals that add meaning and a sense of purpose to the team's work. The vision is a "coming together" or alignment of expectations about how to proceed.

It usually includes the process of working together, the team's operating norms, and the team's result or product. The vision is a step into the collective future. It is built on idealism and expectation because is a hoped-for reality.

The vision held by the team challenges team members to aspire to the very best… to raise the bar on the team's product.

*The vision is different from the common purpose created in the Forming stage.*

| Purpose | Vision |
|---------|--------|
| Why the group exists | What the future can be |

According to Burt Nanus, author of *Visionary Leadership*[1], the following forces are unleashed when the right vision:

▶ Attracts commitment and energizes people

▶ Creates meaning in worker's lives

▶ Establishes a standard of excellence

▶ Bridges the present and the past

[1] Nanus, B. (1995). *Visionary Leadership: Creating a Compelling Sense of Direction for your Organization*. San Francisco, CA: Jossey-Bass Inc.

## *When Vision Isn't Clear*

How do you know when your vision isn't clear or doesn't have buy-in from the team? Here are several indicators:

▶ Is there evidence of confusion about the future, such as frequent disagreements about team priorities? Do meetings have an unfocused or scattered quality about them, seeming to jerk from one thought to another?

▶ Are team members lifeless when you're together? Do they complain about lack of challenge or indicate that they dread getting together because they're not having fun anymore? Are they cynical or pessimistic about the project?

▶ Is the team losing legitimacy in the organization?

▶ Is the team out of tune with developments or trends in the organization?

▶ Is there excessive risk avoidance, with team members sticking to narrow descriptions of their roles, unwilling to accept responsibility or ownership for team projects? Do they resist change?

▶ Does the team lack a shared sense of progress or momentum on the project?

▶ Is there an overactive rumor mill? Do people constantly work on their issues outside of the team instead of confronting them openly and successfully within the team?

# *When Vision Is Hard to Establish*

Here are some forces that can hinder a team's effort to establish a clear vision:

▶ Over-emphasis on task

▶ Assuming the goal is obvious

▶ Personal bias toward independence

▶ Failure to recognize vision's importance

### Over-Emphasis on Task

The desire to immediately become productive can seduce a group into grabbing the first and most apparent symptom and its seemingly obvious solution. Following an intense (and often unfocused) flurry of activity, the group fails, or discovers they have made no real impact. Sadly, this is often chalked up as another piece of evidence that teams don't work rather than recognizing it as example of ineffective or misguided attempts at teamwork.

### Assuming the Goal Is Obvious

Just as multiple witnesses to an event later describe it in different ways, each member of a team perceives the desired outcome of the team's efforts from a unique, personally biased perspective. While the perceptions may be related, they will rarely line up in a highly focused, closely aligned set of blueprints for the final outcome of the team's efforts. A true clarity of vision results only from committed discussion about desired outcomes. Members must willingly confront differences and strive to create consensus.

### Personal Bias toward Independence

Our culture was built on the survival of the fittest—the idea that if you are smart and work hard enough, you can do it on your own. Our organizational reward systems have traditionally been geared toward promotions, bonuses, and raises based on each person's ability to produce outcomes as individuals. Blending into a team and supporting others in pursuit of a mutual goal requires participation, interdependence, and mutual trust. This is a significant shift in stance and can be extremely uncomfortable for individuals who believe the only way to get anything done is to do it yourself. Arriving at a commonly held vision and truly working as a team require discussion, debate, disagreement, conflict, and compromise. Trying to arrive at a common vision can be a painful, lengthy process for individuals who need to feel in control, are inflexible, are used to having their own way, or are simply uncomfortable sharing thoughts and feelings with others.

## Failure to Recognize Vision's Importance

Some team members may hold the common misconception that efforts to clarify the team vision are a waste of time. These views might be expressed directly during a team meeting. More often they are expressed indirectly through a lack of participation or other disruptive behavior. These views might push the team through this necessary step in its development prematurely, with a poorly developed vision. Of course, individuals who feel this way will have no commitment to the vision because they have little or no stake in it, often after having withheld their full participation. The team risks languishing in unfocused efforts with members who at best make half-hearted attempts to help the team succeed. But the team that has Re-Formed and moved past their Storming stage is ready to take on the challenge of a new vision.

"Why are Bob's ideas always called 'concepts',
while mine are called 'notions'?"

# *Dimensions of a Team's Vision*

## Focus

In the process of determining your vision focus, you will clarify some of the following questions for your team.

▶ What was the team's original directive?

▶ What is our purpose?

▶ What do we want?

▶ What does success look like?

## Key Questions

These can help the team clarify its vision focus.

▶ Who are our most important internal and external customers?

▶ What are their top three to five priorities?

▶ What are the key threats the team faces in pursuit of those expectations?

▶ Considering these expectations and threats, what do you most want the team to produce? What's possible? What breakthroughs are possible?

▶ What realities do we have to face? For example, are there physical or geographic boundaries, resource limitations, time constraints, and so on?

## Future Context

This aspect of the vision is based on the realization that nothing remains the same as the team moves to fulfill its purpose. Future context anticipates what to think and do to fulfill the team purpose and achieve its vision.

▶ What changes can be expected in the needs and wants served by the team in the future?

▶ What changes can be expected in the major customers/stakeholder groups served in the future?

▶ What changes can be expected in the economic environments in the future?

▶ What changes can be expected in any external environments that could affect the team's work (social, political, technological, and so on)?

## Coaching Others in Creating Their Vision

According to Peter Block, three qualities to look for in vision statements are:

▶ It should come from the heart.

▶ It should be clear.

▶ The team should take full responsibility for making the transformation.

A team vision is a value-based word picture that helps team members and stakeholders see what the team is trying to accomplish. It is an image (an expression of our collective imagination) of what we hope will be. Like the picture on the box of a jigsaw puzzle, it focuses and directs the team's effort. It may be represented as a word picture (rich in texture with values and emotion-laden words), as a slogan, a team logo, a metaphor, or some combination of these. It represents the ideal—the best hopes of the team. It describes what the team is trying to accomplish and what success looks like. The vision is an essential ingredient of the team formula to achieve sustained high performance.

With the new vision comes the energy that will move this inactive team into the Performing stage. The vision gives them a renewed spirit and sense of team. They may need to be reminded of the importance of keeping the vision current once they have met the current goals and ask themselves, "What's next?"

> **❝** *...to lead others requires that one enlist the emotions of others to share a vision as their own."*
>
> **–Henry M. Boettinger, retired director**
> **of corporate planning, AT&T**

# The New Virtual Team

Even small businesses are now global. Craft shops to car factories buy supplies from India and Japan. We buy from and sell to countries we hadn't heard of five years ago. But with high travel costs and fewer employees we need to find ways to keep people at their desks and yet still connected to the world. All the stages of team development are just as important to the virtual team as to the new, problem, or tired team. One of the special issues that the virtual team faces is that the members often never see faces. In addition there are differences of language, time zones, holidays, cultural norms, and business norms.

## *Virtual Team: Pre-Forming Stage*

If at all possible, the team should have their first meeting in person. If they are coming long distances it can be a meeting that covers Forming, Storming, and Norming. If a gathering isn't an option, then the leader will need to do some "Pre-Forming" work. You'll want to consider:

▶ Technology

▶ Introductions

▶ Team learning

### Technology

Make sure that the right equipment is always available, in working condition, and that everyone has been trained to use it properly.

### Introductions

Without face-to-face meetings, it is important to the visually inclined people on the team to have photos of all participants. Some team members don't need this but for those who do it's a simple pre-forming task. If you use video technology the photos are less important but still nice to have.

Another part of the introductions should include biographies that list years on the job, expertise, role in the company, particular interest in this project or mission, and personal information if appropriate to this team.

**Team Learning**

It may be useful with this team to share information about the stages of team development and how you intend to move quickly past the stages due to the nature of the team. Sending all the team members copies of the organization's mission and vision and their assignment will help them prepare for the first meeting.

## Forming the Virtual Team

The first meeting, like the new team's first meeting, focuses on helping members learn who else is on the team. If they have read bios in advance it will be easier to get acquainted. It is important at this first meeting to set up times and to identify communication problems that may exist around language or culture. It is helpful to have a list of organization and team jargon that needs to be known by all. Conversation about scheduling may include holidays in each country involved.

At this first meeting, review the nature of the team's assignment. What is the team being asked to deliver? Does the team have the expertise and resources to do that? How will this work support the larger organization's vision and strategy?

A conversation about each team member's comfort and experience with virtual teams can help the group understand the needs of the others.

## Storming with the Virtual Team

Just because they can't see each other's faces doesn't mean team members can't storm. All they have to do to show their dissatisfaction is to hang up the phone or turn off the machine, or to allow themselves to be distracted by other people or work in their rooms. To avoid the Storming phase as much as possible, begin each meeting with a check-in.

▶ How is your interview with the COO coming, Camille?

▶ Jonah, what issues did you think we could help you with today?

▶ Is the deadline we set still do-able or do we need to rethink that?

Try to anticipate the concerns that can turn into Storming. It's hard to be aware of concerns when you can't see facial expressions and body language, so you will have to listen carefully to the words and tone.

## *Performing with the Virtual Team*

Bringing all the pieces of the work together to deliver the product requires some extra effort. It is helpful to have someone in your office who can coordinate the information that needs to be sent out and brought together. You will need someone who is dedicated to this service and is a part of the team.

## *Adjourning the Virtual Team*

You might think that this stage is unimportant because the team members haven't been in the same room with each other. But relationships do become important. Some of the members of your virtual teams may become life-long friends so the adjourning shouldn't be ignored.

Congratulate the team on the work they accomplished. Let each one share what they felt was most interesting, successful, and fun about the work, and what they think they learned from the experience. Record what the team has learned about virtual teams because this can be useful for future projects.

Ask the process owner to be present at this Adjourning stage to thank the team for their unusual and successful experience.

# The Intact Team

There is one more type of team that is the combination of all the others. The Intact team works together in a department or organization for years and never really adjourns as a team. They just keep Forming, Storming, Norming, and Performing throughout their time together. A new leader is hired and has to be introduced to the team and they are Re-formed. New organizational rules are set down and the team has to Re-Norm. That may cause friction that leads to Re-Storming. With a strong and knowledgeable leader each change requires a short review of the Forming, Storming and Norming stages and soon a Re-Performing team is in place. Environmental changes such as new leadership, organizational growth and restructuring, or down-sizing may all cause groups to redo these stages. Understanding the stages will give the team a better chance for success.

# Building a High Performance Team

Teams don't just happen, they are built. They require leadership that understands that not everyone thinks alike and that thinking differently is exactly what makes teams innovative, creative, and energetic.

The following are tips that a team leader or member can use to move a team to a higher performance level.

- ▶ Identify purpose and vision.
- ▶ Over-communicate.
- ▶ Be approachable.
- ▶ Build rapport.
- ▶ Fully delegate.
- ▶ Lead by example.
- ▶ Provide feedback.
- ▶ Offer rewards.
- ▶ Encourage growth.
- ▶ Celebrate accomplishments.

### Identify Your Team Purpose and Then Develop a Vision

Each team needs to be clear about the role they play in the success of the organization. Their purpose might not change much from year to year. The accounting department knows what is expected of it and works to make sure they don't let anyone down.

The vision sets clear expectations for what each team can accomplish. The vision helps identify challenging, inspiring goals for a team to achieve.

All team members should help write this team vision. Have the team's purpose and vision statements professionally printed and posted in the work place for all to see.

### Over-communicate

Be certain that your people know what is going on corporate-wide. Share both successes and failures of the team. Keep your team updated about new products, new customers, new business partnerships, and so on.

Inform them of everything from changes in employee benefits to changes in corporate mission or goals. The more knowledge employees have, the better they can identify with an organization.

If you make an error, tell them too much, rather than too little. Individuals don't feel as is they are an important part of a team if the leader keeps them in the dark most of the time.

## Be Approachable

Make certain that people feel comfortable coming to you with problems. A breakdown in communication can be a death sentence to a team. Even the best team leader can't correct a problem he or she doesn't know exists.

Present yourself as a resource. Be there to help, to coordinate, and to run interference for team members when necessary. Be a sounding board if someone needs to discuss an idea or a problem.

In addition, walk around, ask questions, and show interest and concern. You are also a learner. Don't sit in your office and wait for team members to come to you.

## Build Rapport

Plan a short stand-up meeting each morning before the start of the work day. When something changes or when new information arrives, keeps people informed. Give people all of the information they need to perform their current jobs and enough to look ahead and anticipate future opportunities for the team.

Give team members a feeling that they are ahead of the industry curve.

Have occasional informal off-site meetings. Encourage team members to enjoy themselves and get to know one another at these meetings.

## Fully Delegate

You may well be the expert in your field. Perhaps no one else on the entire team knows as much as you do. But respect and use the expertise of your team players.

A high performance team has members who can assume responsibility and make decisions independently. To do this effectively, they must be allowed the opportunity to learn by doing.

People respond in amazing ways when they are given control over the work they do. If asked, most employees can provide several suggestions on how to improve work flow. The more control you give your people over their own areas, the more ownership they feel, the more interest they have, and the harder they try.

## Lead by Example

You can't motivate team members to feel good about their work if you, as their leader, don't. Similarly, team members won't feel ownership or go the extra mile if you don't. You must set an example by demonstrating passion about your work and displaying confidence in the team to do a good job.

### Provide Feedback

Tell your people how they are doing in a timely manner—not six months after the fact. There is no stronger motivator or modifier of behavior than immediate positive or negative reinforcement.

### Offer Rewards

Consider nonmonetary awards such as: public acknowledgement, increased responsibility, status, titles, work space, special parking place close to the door, and so on. Praise your people in public and discipline them in private.

### Encourage Growth

Encourage people to develop personally and professionally. Suggest training programs, books, and journal articles they can read to eliminate weaknesses and fine-tune strengths.

### Celebrate Accomplishments

Share good news. Have a party. Make noise about it. Let everyone know when the team or a team member does something really noteworthy.

Keep the criticisms to a minimum and let praise flow freely.

# Part Summary

## A Word of Encouragement

What can you offer every team you have the opportunity to lead? What knowledge, skills, experience, and talents do you bring to them?

► You know how to put together a good team or create a good team from one already in place, but lacking in essential skills.

► You know how to create a strong purpose statement that helps the team understand what they give to the larger organization.

► You know how to inspire a vision of how that team can be successful.

► You know how to bring people together to accomplish more than any one of them thought possible.

# A P P E N D I X

# Additional Reading

Block, P. *The Empowered Manager: Positive Political Skills at Work.* Jossey-Bass. 1987.

Hirshberg, J. *The Creative Priority: Driving Innovative Business in the Real World.* Harper. 1998.

Johnson, D., & Johnson, F. *Joining Together: Group Theory and Group Skills.* Prentice-Hall. 1991. Another "oldie but goodie" (my copy is held together by tape), that successfully integrates readable social psychology with practical team exercises.

Katzenbach, J., & Smith, D. *The Wisdom of Teams.* Harvard Business Press, 1992. The new "classic" that studied 50 teams in 30 organizations and found that the one clear distinguishing factor in high performing teams was clear performance objectives.

Larson, C., & LaFasto, F. *Teamwork: What Must Go Right/What Can Go Wrong.* Sage Publications. 1989. The authors identified eight characteristics of effective teams and then tested them with a very diverse group of 32 real-life teams such as a college football team, a Mt. Everest expedition, an IBM PC team, a theater production, and a Presidential cabinet.

Mohrman, S., Cohen, S., & Mohrrman, A. *Designing Team-Based Organizations.* Jossey-Bass. 1995. The best book around on the structure and systems required for the strategic deployment of teams.

Moran, L., Musselwhite, E., & Zenger, J. *Keeping Teams on Track.* McGraw-Hill. 1996. Here's a practical guidebook for organizations that are several years into teams and need help on how to deal with issues faced by mature teams.

Nanus, B. *Visionary Leadership.* Jossey-Bass. 1992.

Napier, J., & Gershenfeld, M. *Groups: Theory and Experience.* Wadsworth Publishing. 2001. If you can still find this book, you'll love the authors' clear explanation of group dynamics (e.g., communication, norms, membership, leadership) and advice for practitioners on how to apply the knowledge to the facilitation of teams.

Orsburn, J., Moran, L., Musselwhite, & E., Zenger, J. *Self-Directed Work Teams.* McGraw-Hill. 1990. The first book to make sense of the challenges faced by organizations attempting to implement self-directed teams.

# 50-Minute™ Series

If you enjoyed this book, we have great news for you.
There are more than 200 books available in the
*Crisp Fifty-Minute™ Series*.

## Subject Areas Include:

*Management and Leadership*
*Human Resources*
*Communication Skills*
*Personal Development*
*Sales and Marketing*
*Accounting and Finance*
*Coaching and Mentoring*
*Customer Service/Quality*
*Small Business and Entrepreneurship*
*Writing and Editing*

For more information visit us online at

## www.CrispSeries.com